Communicator's Companion

Devotions for Speakers and Writers

Jean Wise

2nd Expanded and Updated Edition

Previously published as
The Great Communicator: Reflections for Speakers and
Writers

"Writing, the art of communicating thoughts to the mind through the eye, is the great invention of the world...enabling us to converse with the dead, the absent, and the unborn, at all distances of time and space."

- Abraham Lincoln

"Words are, of course, the most powerful drug used by mankind."

-Rudyard Kipling

"Speak clearly, if you speak at all; carve every word before you let it fall."

-Oliver Wendell Holmes

Communicator's Companion Bonus!

Writers and speaker love words. Words are our tools, our bread and butter, the material of our message. We love the swirling taste of a great word on our lips and how the perfect phrase reverberates in another's heart and mind.

I have created a list of wonderful whimsical words I love and compiled them into a **FREE** bonus printable for you.

It's easy to get:
Go to http://healthyspirituality.org/words
Put in the secret password: WORDS
Click to get your inspiration bonus download.
Enjoy my gift to you!

Introduction

I didn't plan on becoming a communicator. Public speaking never entered my mind as a way of serving God. I did love writing, but along that path when I was a teenager I felt God calling me first into nursing.

In my early 20's, no one in our local service group would volunteer to take part in a nearby speaking contest. Shrugging my shoulders, I said I would try.

I won.

Then I won the district contest. Then the regional. And you got it: I came in first at the state competition.

Me, a speaker? I didn't see that coming. And what fun I had. This newfound role as a communicator was empowering and I felt like God was inviting me into a new adventure. I could make a difference in the lives of others and maybe draw them closer to God through my words.

Later, God gave me opportunities to use the written word, too.

Yet I had a lot to learn. I read books on writing and speaking. I attended conferences. I found the experts. I looked to others as role models. These more knowledgeable and experienced people taught me much in the communication field.

But I never studied God as a communicator. He is the Great Communicator. What a role model for us to follow. He is the communicator's Companion.

I invite you to come along with me as I explore what God can show us as he reveals himself in the different aspects of communication. Let's wonder what God would do as a blogger. What would we learn studying God as a presenter? I wonder what new insights we could find imagining God as an agent?

I wrote the first edition of these devotionals in 2012. "The Great Communicator" contained twenty devotions for speakers and writers. As I continue to grow as a communicator I knew it was time to update and lengthen this text.

The Communicator's Companion is this expanded version of the original work and now offers 40 devotions and a fresh title and book cover. My prayer is its words will bless you in your work to share God's message.

I didn't plan on becoming a communicator. But God had that in mind. Now he invites us to learn from him – the Great Communicator and a Companion for everyone.

Communicator

The voice of the Lord is powerful; the voice of the Lord is majestic. Psalm 29:4

Wanted: The Perfect Communicator -an excellent writer who can also move audiences when speaking and an inspirational speaker who can powerfully motivate readers with the written word. If you excel in both areas, you are the communicator for us!

We enter the world of communication usually gifted either in writing or speaking. As we grow in this industry, we are shocked to learn we need to develop skills and experience in both arenas.

At writing conferences across the country, we hear publishers and editors say they want writers who can speak. Speaking associations promote writing a book to supplement the presenter's message.

But publishers, editors, and committees looking for wonderful speakers are not the only ones with this want ad in mind. God is also seeking powerful and inspirational communicators for his kingdom.

What does a powerful and majestic communicator look like? How do we impact lives? How do we develop a writing and speaking voice that reflects God majesty and power? If you were the person on the other side of the desk seeking the right person for a job, what characteristics are important for you?

Lord I want to be a communicator modeled after you.

As a speaker and writer, I struggle with these questions. But Psalm 29 provides an explanation of God's voice and insight that answers his call for communicators.

This psalm describes the voice of the Lord as powerful and majestic, powerful enough to impact and motivate lives and majestic to expand the audience's vision for a wider view of the world. These are two key characteristics of a good communicator.

God models power in his communication style throughout the Bible. I wondered, "When was the first time God's voice was is heard in the Bible? I bet that was a powerful moment." Wouldn't you know it, it is right after the apple scene in the garden. It didn't take long for God to speak up after Adam and Eve disobeyed his voice.

 "Then the man and his wife heard the sound of the Lord God as he was walking in the garden in the cool of the day, and they hid from the Lord God among the trees of the garden. But the Lord God called to the man, "Where are you?" (Genesis 3: 8-9)

God didn't scream, rant, and rave. He didn't preach right from wrong. He didn't use fancy tricks, like thunder and earthquakes, to prove he was powerful and in charge. God demonstrated power by simply walking among the people he created.

As a communicator, we walk with the audience. We come alongside them where they are without an uppity attitude full of teaching or preachy authority. To be a powerful communicator means to connect with and motivate the audience through inspirational stories, emotional examples, and strong images.

We invite the reader and the listener to join us for a while, like companions together on a journey. We are honest with them, sharing our vulnerabilities, struggles, and joys. When they connect, and trust the writer and speaker, their hearts open to God's powerful message.

The majesty of God's voice breaks through when he asks Adam and Eve a simple question, "Where are you?" God knew where they were; they were the ones who were lost. Like a homing beacon, his straightforward, direct, and non-judgmental question drew them to him.

A few years ago, while driving on a non-descript interstate, my mind raced back and forth with upcoming plans. My drifting thoughts abruptly stopped when my car lost all its power. I slowly pulled over to the side of the road and dialed my cell phone for assistance. The tow company's first question was "What is your location?"

I knew the name of the interstate, but paid no attention to my exact location. I needed a mile marker. Like Adam and Eve, I was lost and confused.

As the Great Communicator, God's majestic voice pinpoints our location and provides directions for our journey. So often we go blindly through life, rushing by road signs, and losing direction. Inspirational speakers and writers give mile markers. We come alongside the audience saying, "Let's pay attention to where we are in life and open our eyes beyond our current perspective."

As speakers and writers, our job is to inspire the audience by focusing their attention on God as their mile marker. his majestic and powerful spirit awakens their attention, expands their vision, and leads to transformation.

God is the Great Communicator. He places a want-ad in our hearts, draws us closer to him, and asks us to reflect him through our words. I am learning as part of his call as a speaker and writer to model his voice. To answer this want-ad is to use our words to motivate people by walking alongside them and to inspire them with mile markers that always point the way to God.

Lord, teach me how to be a better communicator. When you talk with us, your power impacts lives and your majesty transforms hearts. As your communicator, that is also my desire.

1. What came first for you – speaking or writing? Which one is your strength? If you don't do one, what could you do to learn more?

2. How did you develop or how are you developing both areas?

3. Where is God inviting you to grow?

4. How do you as a speaker and writer walk alongside the audience and give mile markers?

5. Ask the Lord to open your eyes to discover one new way to impact the lives and transform the hearts of your audience.

Writer

This is what the Lord the God of Israel says:
Write in a book all the words I have spoken to
you. Jeremiah 30:2

Finally, two articles published in one month with my byline. After months of slow progress, my self-confidence plummeting, two magazines accepted my submissions.

I shared my good news with my online writer's group, writing in the email, "I am excited about the first one because the credit makes me look like a real writer. Now getting a second acceptance, I actually feel like I may be really fooling other people into thinking I am a writer."

What is wrong with me? I AM a writer…aren't I? Why don't I feel like I deserve the title? Why am I overwhelmed by this nagging sense of inadequacy?

I retired a few years ago from a high-pressured public job. I knew my role clearly as did others. I based my self-esteem on my occupation. Now when people ask, "What are you doing since you retired," I answer with a great deal of hesitation, "I am a freelance writer."

I fully expect them not to believe me. I imagine them bursting out with wild laughter. you? Prove it. My critics sneer as they drag me into a make-believe court. After a quick trial, they convict me of calling myself something I am not. "GUILTY – not a writer," screams the judge as he slams his gavel.

Ok Lord, now what? Why am I even spending time and energy with this? Am I afraid to fail? I focus on the end product and I cannot even get started. Forgive me Lord for wasting precious time and gifts you have given me. Show me what you want me to do next. God, you are a writer, please help me.

God told Jeremiah to "write in a book all the words I have spoken to you." What is God saying to me in this verse? I need to listen to his words, not the inner critics. God speaks and fills me with energizing hope. The inner critics fill me with distracting doubt. When I listen only to God, it helps me focus on my writing and quiets the disruptions and discouragements. Listening prayer and meditation reminds me who is in charge and who is leading me.

God gently reminds me I am his child. Reassured that my identity is firmly rooted in his unconditional love, he fills me with the strength and the resolve to return to my call to write. We are created in his image, even his image as a writer. "What am I? I am myself a word spoken by God," writes Thomas Merton.

God, the writer, calls to me to follow him as a writer. how do I imitate God in this role? He wrote! He did not doubt; he took action. Even Jesus did not worry about his self-image. He just focused on being obedient to his call.

Where do I start? "In his heart a man plans his course, but the Lord determines his steps" (Proverbs 16:9). Obedience comes when I take the next step I believe God has shown me and I act. I need to focus my energies on the next project before me.

When we falter, it helps to remember who we are, who called us, and to take one step in response to our call. To learn what to do and where he wants me to spend the time and gifts he gave me, I need to listen, remember who I am, and to act.

At what point will I believe I am a writer? Do the number of books I sell, the articles with my byline or even being published at all, define my success? There will be a time when I am no longer confused by my new role as a writer and can confidently shout to the world, "hey I <u>am</u> a writer?"

God the writer will lead me to the next step. My writing path is in his hands whether I am ever published or not. I will focus only on him, lean on his strength and guidance, and know he loves me as his child. Who am I? I am his child who tries to imitate him as a writer. I tell my inner critics the only proof they will ever see is my obedience to my calling. I am a writer!

Dearest Lord, I struggle so with knowing if I am where you want me. I am like an uncertain child constantly looking for reassurance. Lord I do believe, help my unbelief! I do believe I am where you want me, doing what you want me to do. I do believe I am a writer. help me believe it in my heart.

1. Write out your name and title.

2. What title is on the nameplate of your desk?

3. Imagine someone asks you what you do. Write out your answer, and say it aloud.

4. How do you define success as a communicator?

5. How is God calling you as a communicator? What is your next step?

Planter of Thoughts

I am the true vine, and my Father is the gardener.
John 15: 1

God is the creator.

Not me. Not you. God is the one who created the world out of nothing. He formed the beauty in a sunset. He designed the vastness in the universe and the intricacies of the human cell.

God plants ideas, visions, and illustrations into the imaginations of communicators so we can spread his message of love to all.

Creative Lord, may I always remember you are my muse and my creative inspiration.

In most ancient cultures, creativity was considered a divine characteristic. Creative communicators love to connect and be inspired by this muse, this spirit, this Holy Spirit.

The origin of the writer/speaker muse comes from Greek mythology. The nine daughters of Zeus ruled over different domains of creativity, such as poetry, hymns, dance, and music. They were called the muses and became guiding spirits for artists.

As Christians, we know all ideas come from God through the Holy Spirit.

William Blake wrote, "I myself do nothing. The Holy Spirit accomplishes all through me."

Johannes Brahms gives the source of his creativity: "Straightaway the ideas flow in upon me, directly from God."

As Christian communicators, when we approach a blank screen, empty paper, or new presentation, we bow before the Holy Spirit and ask her help in creating the words to best tell God's story.

Just as God brought order out of chaos and birthed the world, he takes our open hearts and minds as his new canvas. A formless idea takes shape, a note explodes into a melody, and one word blossoms into a book. We receive and gather the vision and ingenuity that God grows and nourishes in our imagination.

As speakers and writers, we bow down before the Creator and acknowledge he is the source of all ideas. He is the planter of thoughts and the gardener of innovation.

Lord of all Creativity, we know all thoughts, words, and art begins in your heart. Inspire us with your spirit. Walk alongside us as we communicate. Open our ears to hear your wisdom. Thank you for taking us along on this journey to spread your good news and helps us always to remember it is about you and not us.

1. Have you ever invited the Holy Spirit to create art with you?
2. How do you welcome the Holy Spirit into your work?

3. Describe a time when you knew/felt/experienced something outside of you, leading your creativity.

Poet

My heart bursts its banks, spilling beauty and goodness. I pour it out in a poem to the king, shaping the river into words. Psalm 45:1 (The Message)

Poets dance with words.

Writers gather words together, then sprinkled them with rhythm and rhyme. Speakers pause for dramatic effects and change the pitch of their voices to draw audiences into the story. We want our readers and listeners to hum along with the cadence materializing in their eyes, their ears, and their hearts.

Communicators know to listen to the heartbeat of language and respond to its tiniest movement. A poet lives inside every communicator.

We inhale life's experiences and exhale meaningful poems.

Whether we call ourselves poets or not, when we weave expressions together that pierce the hearts and minds of our audiences – we become poets.

Lord I want my words – whether spoken or written- to spill over with beauty and goodness, pointing ever to you. Poetry is one of your strongest keys to truth and wisdom.

Robert Browning wrote, "God is the perfect poet."

When we open our hearts to the Lord, his joy, his words, his message bursts forth from our voices. God's poetry becomes our poetry. As communicators, the more we dwell in his writing, his holy scriptures, the more our words are rooted in his message.

We fill up on his words in the Bible; our words gain strength and life.

"Poetry is an echo, asking a shadow to dance," Carl Sandberg wrote.

Isn't that a great expression? To echo and imitate God's words in our writing and speaking? We live that way – shadows of the sacred, reflections of the King.

The words we work so hard to put together are but a weak reflection of God's vocabulary.

When we approach our work, let's begin as poets. First take to the Bible, not just reading, but soaking in its meaning and allow it to transform our hearts. We slowly read each word pausing at the one that resonate with us. What does it mean to us? Why is God inviting me to sit with this word today?

Allow yourself to hear the divine music inviting you to swing and sway.

Next, we soak each word we speak or write in prayer. A poet scrutinizes each meaning, every nuance to find the best-polished word. *God, is this really what you want me to express in this paragraph?*

Then we offer our work into God's hands for blessing. God will take our scribbles, our simple attempts, and he will magnify them for his purpose.

Imagine what poetry we will hear in heaven.

Lord of all lyrics and lines, what I communicate is mere shadow of your greatness. I ask that you come alongside me as I write and speak so the vibration of my words echo deep in the hearts of others. Holy Spirit, I know you have the power to help me discover just how you want me to express your message. My heart and ears are open to you.

1. Write a poem today expressing how you feel about your gifts as a communicator.

2. Think about your creative process as you begin to write or formulate a presentation, what can you do to hear God's music better?

3. Find some of your favorite poems. Why do they resonate with you? how could you incorporate than into your speaking and writing?

4. What word did God give you today? Did you dance with it?

Compiler

Oh, that my words were recorded, that they were written on a scroll Job 19:23

Ever notice the court recorder? He or she sits silently on the side of the judge, chronicling all the words spoken in that room. The documents are detailed, defined and often dramatic. A court reporter must be descriptive, diligent, and direct.

These highly skilled professionals listen carefully to the proceedings and compile all the communication taking place. They are creating legal documents that support cases and may determine someone's guilt or innocence in a trail. Their words authenticate what has happened within that courtroom and they record what people share about what their experiences.

Lord, may all my communication be as clear and correct as a court reporter's.

The creed of a court reporter is interesting to read:

"My profession stems from humanity's desire and its necessity to preserve the happenings of yesterday and tomorrow.
"My profession was born with the rise of civilization in Ancient Greece.
"I was known as a scribe in Judea, Persia, and the Roman Empire.
"I preserved the Ten Commandments for posterity and was with King Solomon while building the temple.

"I was with the founding fathers of the United States when they drafted the Declaration of Independence. My hand labored upon the scroll that set forth the Bill of Rights.

"The immortal Abraham Lincoln entrusted me to record the Emancipation Proclamation.

"I was commissioned to be with Roosevelt at Yalta. I was with Eisenhower on D-Day and with MacArthur at Tokyo.

"I have kept confidence reposed with me by those in high places, as well as those in lowly places.

"My profession protects the truthful witness, and I am a nemesis of the perjurer. I am a party to the administration of justice under the law and the court I serve.

"I discharge my duties with devotion and honor.

"Perhaps I haven't made history, but I have preserved it through the ages.

"In the past I was called a scribe. Today I am the court reporter who sits in the courts of my country and in the United States Congress.

"I am the verbatim court reporter."

Author Unknown

When we write and prepare a talk, we listen deeply to God. We try our best to hear his words and "discharge our duties with devotion and honor."

God guides us as communicators and blesses us with his wisdom and words. Our job is to listen and record his word and become court reporters for the Lord.

Dear Lord and Judge of all, open our ears to hear you clearly and accurately. Give us courage to record your message and to share it with others. May we always serve you with devotion and honor.

1. How well do you write with such attention to detail?
2. How well do you listen to God when planning a presentation?
3. What word in the Court Reporter Creed stands out to you?

Novelist

Listen, dear friends, to God's truth, bend your ears to what I tell you. I'm chewing on the morsel of a proverb; I'll let you in on the sweet old truths, Stories we heard from our fathers, counsel we learned at our mother's knee. We're not keeping this to ourselves, we're passing it along to the next generation—God's fame and fortune, the marvelous things he has done. Psalm 78:2 (The Message)

Don't you love getting drawn into a good story? You stay up all night, turning each page with anticipation, vowing you will go to bed at the end of the next chapter, but you can't close the book. Suddenly you look at the clock and can't believe hours have passed.

Novelists create characters, settings, and dialogue you can see and hear in your mind and in your heart. We befriend the characters we like and develop strong feelings about the ones we distrust. We learn to know all their unique traits. With impatience, we wait for the next book so we can spend more time with our new friends.

A good novel has a universal truth, something every reader identifies with and wants to believe in. Sometimes this clear reality is easy to spot; other times we dig deep into the story to find its foundation.

Stories share a common model: a beginning, a middle, and an end. At first, the novelist introduces the reader to the characters placed in an interesting setting. Then conflict arises.

Each story builds its tale through an intriguing series of complications, obstacles, and crises. In the end, the ultimate crisis is resolved.

Novelists weave complex sagas together like an expert seamstress with colorful background stories. They add substance and a touch of mystery to their work.

Lord, I want to be drawn into your story too. You are the writer of the greatest story.

I never thought of God being a novelist before. He IS the story – the truth our hearts know is real.

God, the grandest novelist of all, creates us as his unique characters and places us into his settings. If we let go of our worldly expectations, we can be drawn into his story and watch it unfold before us.

He weaves his word into our hearts.

He places us against his back-story, a foundation full of characters such a David, Joseph, and Peter. God adds depth to our tales by adding other people's narratives, both living and dead, people we read about and people we know.

God, the novelist, creates the perfect story arc. He established a strong dramatic beginning, fashioning the world and each of us out of chaos into life.

God adds enough conflict to help us learn and grow and to arrive at the finale at just the precise moment as he, the Author, desires.

He stays with us through each twist and turn and up and down of our journey.

He has already told us the ending. Our ultimate crisis is facing our death and coming home to him at last.

God is present now. He holds our past. He shapes our future.

These verses in Psalm 78 call upon us as writers and speakers to continue to tell God's story. Our lives become God's novel. Our job assignment is to pass the good news onto new generations and to communicate the sacred story.

Lord, you are the novelist I want to read. In every moment of my life, may my story reflect your story.

1. How has God the novelist created your story?

2. As this reflection describes God as a novelist, what is your image of God right now?

3. Reflecting where you are in your life, what is God foreshadowing for your future?

4. What conflicts in your life have helped you develop character?

5. Describe the back-story of your life.

Publisher

But regarding anything beyond this, dear friend, go easy. There's no end to the publishing of books, and constant study wears you out so you're no good for anything else. Ecclesiastes 12:12 (The Message)

The statistics are amazing.

Google estimates almost 130 million distinct book titles are published each year. This represents so many books that if you read a book a day, it would take you more than 350,000 years to get through your "to read" pile.

Now with the advent of self-publishing and e-books, the number of books is expected to explode even more. In 2010, Bowker's Reports stated these "nontraditional" books published with ISBNs grew to more than 3 million works.

Anyone can be a publisher in today's world.

Lord, may all that I publish glorify you.

What can we learn from God as publisher? His word in this verse from Ecclesiastes is clear: go easy. We can publish trash, heresies, and even false doctrines if we are not careful.

"Go easy" means to start each talk, each article, and each book idea in prayer. Start with God first.

God instructs us to "go easy." This means to do our research first. Is that quote accurate or just a misquote someone put out onto the Internet? What is the primary source of any information we put into our presentations and our writing?

"Go easy" means not to work all by ourselves, thinking we can do his work entirely on our own. I swallow my pride and send my work to my critique partners and use their feedback to have the best final product for God. Seeking advice from others I ask: Is this the truth? Are my words clear? Do they point to God?

"Go easy" means to write, rewrite, and rewrite some more before pushing the publish button.

It is possible something we publish, either through a traditional publisher or self-publishing, may languish on the shelf and only be read by our faithful friends and a few doting relatives. Maybe our words will only touch one person. That may be God's intention for our work.

Charles Dickens visited America and eventually wrote about his journey in his book *American Notes*. While in Boston, Dickens went to the Perkins Institution and Massachusetts School for the Blind, where he observed Laura Bridgman, a blind and deaf girl, and how she was receiving education there. Dickens wrote about that insignificant incident in his book.

Forty years later Captain Arthur Keller and his wife, Kate, read Dickens' account of Laura Bridgman and the Perkins Institution. The Kellers sought a teacher from that institute to come to their home and train their blind and deaf daughter. The teacher? Anne Sullivan. And the daughter? Helen Keller.

One small story in a book written by Dickens and years later, we still see the impact.

Martin Luther nailed his 99 theses on a church's wooden door in 1517 intending only for his words to spark a little local debate.

But something happened to his words: They were published!

Guttenberg created the printing press more than 60 years before Luther wrote his document. Someone in Wittenberg took his words to a printing press and, as they say, the rest was history.

Publishing is a powerful world-changing concept and one that could be used for good or evil. Following God's word: "go easy" will help us publish for good and for God.

Lord, help us go easy with our written and spoken words. We want what we write and speak to be only in your light and to glorify only you.

1. What does "go easy" mean to you?

2. How do you feel about the growing self-publishing opportunities? Is God inviting you to grow in that area?

3. How do you discern what to research and what to publish?

4. Would you still write and speak if only a few read or heard your words?

Word Painter

"How can we picture God's kingdom? What kind of story can we use? It's like a pine nut. When it lands on the ground, it is quite small as seeds go, yet once it is planted; it grows into a huge pine tree with thick branches. Eagles nest in it." Mark 4:30-32 (The Message)

I failed scissor-cutting in kindergarten. My parents received a note saying I needed more work with my fine motor skills or they might not pass me onto first grade. Funny how memories like this stick with you.

I did go onto first grade, but for most of my life felt that I had little coordination, especially with my small muscles. After all, I can't paint. I can't draw. And my stitches with sewing are loopy and irregular.

So how can I, as Mark asks in today's verse, create pictures of God's kingdom?

Writers are word painters. We reach deep into the dictionary of our minds and the thesaurus of our souls and with the help of the Holy Spirit, portraits of God burst out.

Speakers tell stories that captivate an audience, inspiring their listeners to reach higher or dig deeper into God's words.

Dear Lord, I want to be the kind of writer and speaker that when I am finished the audience thinks, "Yes, she said/wrote just what I was feeling, but I didn't realize it until she said/wrote it." My desire is to use the gifts you have given me to help make you, the invisible, visible.

"The role of a writer is not to say what we all can say, but what we are unable to say." Anaïs Nin

We may not paint, draw, or quilt but we are visual and verbal artists. Our tools are the alphabet. We form images and paintings in the minds of our audience through our arrangements of vowels and consonants.

These verses in Mark tell us to plant the seeds of the pine nut and with God's help, it grows into a huge tree in the hearts of others.

We draw attention to the quiet wonders, the subtle light, and the extraordinary details of this world that all point back to its Creator.

Writers all know the mantra, "Show, don't tell." We work on our craft to improve how we describe a scene, feeling, or character. Speakers search for the right story to illustrate a point or a powerful quote for the audience to easily retain.

I love the saying from Anton Chekhov, "Don't tell me the moon is shining; show me the glint of light on broken glass."

Word painting pushes us to find just the right word. Mark Twain wrote, "The difference between the right word and the almost-right word is the difference between the lightning and the lightning-bug."

We are word painters.

Dear Master Artist, you have called us to be word painters. We draw like kindergartners when we try on our own. With your help and Guiding Spirit, our words spring into colorful murals. May our words only paint portraits of you.

1. When you read about being a word painter, how does that change your attitude and beliefs as a writer/speaker?

2. We may never see the end results of a full-grown tree in the heart of another. Reflect on where you have planted seeds and maybe now, years later, can see results.

3. What do you need to do as a speaker or writers to grow as a word painter?

4. List five ways you as a communicator find just the right word or illustration for your story.

5. Try drawing or sketching a scene from your writing or an image from a presentation. What did you learn?

Source

If any one of you thinks God has something for you to say or has inspired you to do something, pay close attention to what I have written. This is the way the Master wants it. 1 Corinthians 14:37 (The Message)

Journalists learn quickly to confirm the source of the information for their article.

We read the accusing headlines screaming about "fake news." We hear gossip and stories that deep down we know cannot be true. We learn later some of the hearsay that contains some accurate but misleading facts. We are left feeling confused, untrusting, and lost in knowing what is real or not real.

What is the truth? Where do we find it?

Lord, I am confused and at times don't know what to believe anymore. Show me the truth.

God as the Great Communicator is the source of all truth.

If we plant our roots deeply into knowing God, knowing who we are in him, and realigning our hearts focused on him, we will hear his wisdom and know his way.

As communicators, we pay attention to the Master, who is our source of what is genuine and true.

Whenever Jesus faced a difficult crossroads, he withdrew away by himself to spend time with the source. We too can follow this example.

Before facing the cross, Jesus prayed in the Garden of Gethsemane. When entering a difficult time, loaded with volatile emotions and unknown solutions, we pray and trust our source.

Jesus continually returned to the source of all truth, became grounded, realigned with God, and returned to his calling. We too need time to connect with God as children of God and as communicators.

As speakers and writers, we fill our well, our reserve, to persevere by reconnecting to the source of all our work, inspiration, and strength. We connect with our Source of Life through prayer, quiet time with the Lord, journaling, and worship. Intentionally we focus our hearts and minds on the source we have learned to trust.

Journalists' advise to always have two sources to verify the truth. This is called the two-source rule. We are blessed to have three: God, Jesus, and the Holy Spirit.

Let's not struggle in confusion and fear, but keep our connections with our sources of all truth. God is the source.

Dear Master and Source of all truth, continue to lead us in doing your work. Remind us to return to you as the source to verify our words and strengthen our presentations. We want to be our

best for you to glorify you and tell others your
good news.

1. Describe your rhythm and routine of spending time with God.
2. What is working? What needs some improvement?
3. How do you best connect to the Source?

A Communicator's Vision

Then the Lord told me: "I will give you my message in the form of a vision. Write it clearly enough to be read at a glance. Habakkuk 2:2 (Contemporary English Version)

My eyes squinted trying to dim the glaring lights of the approaching car. I clutched the steering wheel praying to stay on my side of the road.

"This is it," I thought. "I must get into the optometrist and get my eyes checked. My sight is definitely worse. I can't see where I am going."

A few days later, I discovered my foolish mistake. I put my contacts in the wrong eyes. No wonder I couldn't see right. Clear vision is essential to knowing where we are going and to correct our direction if we wander off course.

Lord, be my vision. Guide me as I write and speak so others see you and know you better.

Many communicators spend time in creating a vision statement for their ministry. A one or two sentence description about our speaking and writing gives our work meaning and a sense of direction. A vision statement also helps us decide what project to work on next and when to say no to an idea.

Like the verse in Habakkuk tells us, a vision should be clear and be able to read at a glance. A vision plan considers the future.

I like what Evelyn Underhill wrote about vision:

"The most important thing for you is your vision, your sense of that God whom your work must

glorify. The richer, deeper, wider, truer your vision of Divine Reality the more real, rich and fruitful your work is going to be. You must feel the mysterious attraction of God, his loveliness and wonder, if you are ever going--in however simple a way--to impart it to others."

Many communicators enfold this process in prayer. Writing in a journal is one way I found to express what I thought God was saying to me. I pray about those words and then I talk with others. All this helps me hear where he was leading me in the formation of a vision statement.

Questions to consider when discerning a communicator's vision:

• What kind of impact do I see my speaking/writing making on others?

• What is really on my heart to communicate? What is my passion?

• What Bible verses resonate with my dream to speak and write?

• Are there specific words that guide my life?

• Why me? What unique spiritual gift, interest, passions, and stories do I bring to this plan?

When I first envisioned my writing accomplishments in writing, I thought writing a bestseller or receiving a Pulitzer Prize or a Newbery Medal would be part of my vision as a communicator. I imagined being a national expert on something amazing. I thought having speaking engagements with other dignitaries addressing millions on a national stage would be one of my goals. To be fully honest, some of this still tugs at my heart and ego.

But what I discovered through much prayerful listening is this: I want my writing and speaking to honor God, not me. As a communicator, I hope to change lives and hearts, focused on him.

I pray my words draw hearts into the wonder of God. My vision is helping to nurture the sacred within the hearts of others so they sing the song God planted in their souls.

Join Habakkuk and write down the vision that God has planted in your heart. A vision will help you see where you are going and give your communication deeper meaning. It provides a measure to evaluate your progress and a chart that will get you back on course if you wander.

Visionary Lord, guide me in this journey to hear where you want my speaking and writing to go. I do want to glorify you in my work. I want my gifts and talents to honor you. I ask for clarity, wisdom, and a sense of your presence in this discernment ahead.

1. What do you desire to achieve by your speaking and writing?

2. What is really on your heart to communicate?

3. What will be different in your life if you achieved your vision?

4. Ideally, where do you see your ministry in five years?

Footnoter

*Join with others in following my example,
brothers, and take note of those who live
according to the pattern we gave you. Philippians
3:17*

College professors love them and professional
articles require them. Footnotes.

I cringed when I am asked to include them.
Footnotes are the miniscule details, verifying the
sources of many sentences. They are the fine print
at the end of each chapter or the bottom of each
page.

Sometimes I ignore them. At times, I know I
never even notice them. Those tiny words are
invisible to me.

*All-knowing Lord, teach me the lessons found in
taking note of the details in life.*

I have been thinking about footnotes. As a writer,
I dread them because of how time-consuming
they are. These notes demand to be written in a
certain order, according to a submission guideline
or style manual. But as a reader, I love how they
add depth and awareness, like a fine seasoning
adds a tasty nuance to a meal.

Occasionally, I wonder if I am just a footnote to
other people. Ignored. Unnoticed. Not really
needed. An unseen, useless detail.

We are not footnotes in history or in an illustration. We don't clutter at the bottom of the page on life. We are an integral part of God's story and a detailed link needed in his plan. Our story adds shade to the final masterpiece that God is painting. A detail that would lessen the end piece of art if it wasn't included.

Footnotes add value. They are the substance. The nuance. They provide the structure behind the work of the writers. These miniscule details are the research adding depth for the speech.

A footnote provides the insight and background for the message we are communicating. I love the footnotes in my study Bible. Here I find understanding, historical explanations, and new meanings into a word.

Digging deep into a study Bible or reference material strengthens our presentations and writing, even if we don't add footnotes. The background gives us deeper ideas and forms our message.

Now when I see footnotes at the bottom of the page, I appreciate the work that occurred to undergird the message. When I listen to a presentation, I understand the study and research behind the speech that often isn't spoken or shared.

Paul tells the Philippians to take note. To pay attention to the details, they may not otherwise see. As we watch the various aspects of life, we notice the patterns.

As communicators we take note, add notes, and bring notes to the attention of our audience. We are a valuable part of God's format as we add transformational background to further his story in his book of life.

God, you are the writer of all creation. Help us pay attention to the details that add to your good news. Open our minds and hearts to value even the tiniest, overlooked fact that may be exactly what you want us to communicate.

1. What do you value about footnotes?
2. Write in your journal about a time you may have felt like "just a footnote."
3. How are you paying attention to God's footnotes?

Wordsmith

The right word at the right time is like a custom-made piece of jewelry. Proverbs 25:11 (The Message)

Imagine a blacksmith.

A blacksmith is a person who creates objects from iron or steel by forging the metal. he or she uses the tools of the trade to bend, cut and shape the final product. The result is intricate gates, grills, railings, sculptures, tools, and even weapons.

Blacksmiths customize their work by using the right tools for the right job. They use their crucial skills every time in their work.

The blacksmith's basic ingredient is iron. He heats the iron until the metal becomes soft enough to be shaped by the hammer, anvil, and chisel.

Forging shapes the metal by repeated hammering. heating iron to a "forging heat" allows the work to be bent as easily as if it were softer metals such as copper or silver.

Blacksmiths also use a technique called drawing to lengthen or draw out the metal.

Bending is done with the hammer over the horn or edge of the anvil.

When the work is in its final stages, the blacksmith uses a file to remove the sharp edges and emery wheels to polish the surface until it shines.

Lord, use me as a blacksmith of words for your kingdom.

As speakers and writers, we are blacksmiths or wordsmiths for God.

What gives us the power to weld words into the hearts of our readers? Where does the fire start? Our basic tools as wordsmiths are: prayer, patience, patterns, and polish.

Prayer is like the blacksmith's iron – the basic ingredient to our speaking and writing. Our core element, the strength of our words, only comes from an intimate relationship with God. This connection with God is built up by spending time with him in prayer.

Patience resembles the drawing and the over and over again hammering each word and sentence to perfection. Is this the right word? What story best illustrates this point?

Patterns remind us to customize and shape our communication to each audience. Where the blacksmith uses a hammer, anvil, and chisel, we hammer our keyboard and edit our work.

Both blacksmiths and wordsmiths must put the final polish on their work, removing sharp edges. Reading our work aloud and being open to critique finds those rough spots that need improvement.

"Write while the heat is still in you.

The write who postpones the recording of his thoughts uses an iron which has cooled to burn a hole with he cannot inflame the minds of his audience."

Henry David Thoreau

As wordsmiths, we give back the words that the Lord first gave us, forging the finest masterpiece we can create.

Worthy Wordsmith, you are the creator of all words and the supplier of all power. As I try to serve you with my words, send forth your spirit upon me to find just the right words that speak best for you. The best way to say what you want me to communicate. Help me find the finest images to light your way so others can see you, know you and love you more.

1. Write out your creative process and invite God to take control of every aspect of it.

2. List several words that best describe your communication style. Are they the right words or almost the right words? What did you learn?

3. How do the steps of prayer, patience, pattern, and polish apply to your writing, your speaking, and your life?

Bookseller

In all my prayers for all of you, I always pray with joy because of your partnership in the gospel from the first day until now. Philippians 1:4-5

The word "bookseller" first entered our vocabulary in the 15th century. Its use multiplied with the emerging industry of the printing press, and the making of more books available for the public.

Partnerships proliferated between printers and sellers, between the sellers and readers, between the authors and sellers, and between the authors and readers.

A partnership means an associate or joint heir, one who holds "a part or a piece" to share with another and to others.

Partnerships with booksellers provide the link to expand a message from one person to many. The creation from an author or speaker expands and goes beyond the original source.

God of all partnerships, help me see how working with others shares your message throughout the world.

God's good news is about how Jesus came, died, and rose from the dead for us. The great news of how much God loves us and wants a relationship with us is the message that God wants taken throughout the world and into every heart.

Just like booksellers help an author, we partner with God to spread his word to the hearts of others. We honor humbly that this is the work of God, not our own endeavors.

When we communicate through spoken and written word, we partner with the reader and listener. Then this person may mention the thought in a small group or to a family member, casting the seed of God's love into their heart or mind to bloom within their life. What starts with God, circulates, cultivates, and carries God's message beyond our imagination.

God is the original bookseller. He takes his word, his Word, and distributes it to readers, publishers, writers, and speakers. We then become allies, sharing the word with others, partnering with them and distributing his word of hope, joy, and love.

Quite a partnership, isn't it? God and the speaker. God and the writer. God and us, working together.

Lord of all partnerships, we are honored to share your good news with others. Guide our words, open our eyes to new possibilities, and help us find the key partnerships to do your will.

1. How do you see your speaking and writing as a partnership with God?
2. Ponder if you view your ministry as your work or as God's work.
3. How are you spreading the good news today?

Ink

You show that you are a letter from Christ, the result of our ministry, written not with ink but with the Spirit of the living God, not on tablets of stone but on tablets of human hearts. 2 Corinthians 3:3

I keep them safely in an old suitcase in the closet. The papers are fragile, the ink starting to fade, but they hold a special place in my heart. They are three love letters from my dad to my mom written during World War II.

Dad signed each of his letters "ILD," an abbreviation of German words, "I love you." In German I love you is *Ich liebe dich.*

As I was growing up, Dad, a physician, left for work early and was frequently called out in the middle of the night. he usually left mom a note, always signed – "ILD, Johnnie." – Dad's written expression of love.

Though the ink is discolored, the memory of his message of love remains with me today. Dad's ILD may fade, but the story about how much he loved us won't ever go.

Lord, may my words reflect your permanent and penetrating ink into the hearts of people.

Ink is a fascinating medium used to communicate messages. Most of the time it is permanent and can't be erased. you sign your name in ink on legal binding documents since it seldom disappears.

A few months ago, a friend of ours moved his computer printer across his house from the den to the other end of the living room. He didn't notice he dripped a continuous trail of black ink marking his path.

Over the next few weeks, he tried every cleaning product he could find to remove the ink. Each time, the rug looked clean, but by the next morning, the ink reappeared.

Yes, they had to replace the carpet and even seal the boards underneath, so the ink wouldn't seep through.

Ink is permanent and penetrating. The ink in our pens and computers plants powerful phrases of love into the hearts and minds of others.

God's ink – his Holy Spirit – is the same way.

I wonder how I show ILD to others in my writing and in my life?

If I am, as this verse says, to be a letter from Christ, what are others reading when they see my words and actions?

Am I transparent enough for God's spirit to shine through or am I hidden away in a dark trunk?

When I start to write, do I visualize myself as God's ink?

I have always loved the saying from Mother Teresa, "I am a pencil in the hand of God." What a great first step before writing: to see yourself being used by God as his ink. Words from not from my fingers or mouth, but from God's heart.

He is the story - we are his ink.

Lord, fill my heart with permanent ink from your
Holy Spirit. May my words always point to you
and my life reflect your message of love. Help me
inscribe your words on the heart of others so
floods of letters from Christ fill the world.

1. How do you start each time you write? Do you dive into or do you start with prayer?

2. What has God written on your heart?

3. God's ink is permanent on your heart. How does that knowledge change your heart?

Chatterer

The wise in heart accept commands, but a chattering fool comes to ruin. Proverbs 10:8

Remember the Chatty Cathy doll? She was one of most popular dolls in the 1960s and one of the first that could talk. Parents rushed out to buy one for their children.

Pull the string in her back, and she repeated a collection of 10-11 mechanical phrases.

I love you.
May I have a cookie?
I'm hungry.
Please carry me.
Where are we going?

After hours of listening to Chatty Cathy, parents regretted the adoption of this talkative toy.

We all been stuck in situations where we were cornered by a chattering fool. The person who talks nonstop in the airplane. The neighbor you can't get away from once they begin to talk. Maybe we've been cornered by the persistent salesman trying to seal a deal. Or at a party listening to a 20-minute monologue speeding at 90 miles per hour.

Wise Lord, help me learn the difference between a babbling fool and silent sage.

How can we as communicators accept God's commands in our hearts and curb the chattering fool within us?

Knowing when to speak and when to actively listen helps. Intentionally practicing the gift of not speaking or having the last word also works. Choosing our words wisely and honoring the conversation from another fosters open dialogue.

When we invite the Spirit into the conversation, we best keep quiet so she can speak to our hearts in her loving whisper.

I know at times I have been guilty of being the chattering fool. When I am upset, nervous, or defensive, my ego explodes into endless yacking. At these moments, I need to pause and remember that *"The wise in heart accept commands."*

The wise are self-aware of when we are too wordy, taking over conversations. We offer grace to those chattering fools we encountered and pray for the long-winded, listening to what they are trying to say. Perhaps we find wisdom buried beneath the weight of words.

Thinking about the Chatty Cathy doll showed me a lesson. When I reread her phrases, I discovered her sayings could be simple prayers, a lesson I would have never learned if I didn't listen to her chatter. Her phrases matched prayers I have said to God, as a chattering fool:

I love you.
May I have a cookie?
I'm hungry.

Please carry me.
Where are we going?

Wise Lord, thank you for listening to our nonsensical chattering and quieting our hearts to hear your wisdom. Help us say less and listen more. Lead us to choose words wisely and use our mouths to glorify you.

1. When have you been a chattering fool and what triggered you to react that way?
2. Which of the Chatty Cathy phrases match prayers you have made?
3. How can we as communicators accept God's commands in our hearts?

Editor

As iron sharpens iron, so one man sharpens another. Proverbs 27:17

My editor at the local newspaper sends out weekly tips to all the reporters. For example, I learned in the newspaper business, words are sometimes spelled different from normal acceptance.

I cover school board meetings where they hire employees to serve as advisors: yearbook advisors, junior class advisors, and so on. But in the newspaper world, the word advisor is spelled adviser. I didn't know that until the editor pointed this out.

Newspapers follow the AP format style manual and the editor's goal is to have all the newspaper writers following those rules for consistency.

Style manuals are used since more than one writer is contributing work to the newspaper. The finished piece doesn't reflect the personal style of the writer, but the voice of the publication.

My editor is sharpening my skills as a writer, but also improving the writing for the entire newspaper. The editor raises our writing to a higher level.

One of the jobs as an editor is to make the final product the best it can be.

But having "my precious words, my babies" honed to someone else's standard can hurt a little. Polishing my creative work can rub me the wrong way unless I accept that the final product will be better and trust the editor to do what is best. I have to be willing to be vulnerable and place my work into the hands of someone more knowledgeable and one who sees the big picture.

Lord, open my eyes to see your work as an Editor in my life and ministry.

How does God act as our editor?

God uses his sacred stylebook to guide us in how to live and to correct us when we stray. I need to keep his word, the Bible, close at hand for all my work in life.

Just like some words at the newspaper are spelled uniquely, we are expected to live differently as Christians from the rest of the world. The Bible helps us along this path.

In spending time with God in prayer, I learn to trust him to polish my heart to reflect him, not my personal ego. I empty my hands, full of my individual style, based on my self-centered wants, to grasp his will. I give up my voice to become his voice.

God, the Editor, shapes my character when I open my heart, exposing my most vulnerable part, to his love, grace, and mercy.

God takes us as he first created us into his hands. his tender touch wipes off our sins and the smudges of the world and polishes us to perfection – his perfection, his wholeness.

God is the iron that sharpens our lives.

Lord, be my editor. Take my words, my thoughts, my desires and perfect them. you alone know what is best for me. Only you can see the full plan. Even though it hurts at first to be corrected, I know your way is The Way. Help me trust you, knowing you are in charge of the final product, the story of my life and the lives of others. Divine Editor, be the iron that sharpens me.

1. Identify who improves your written and/or communications?

2. When you receive constructive criticism of your work, how does that make you feel? Name those feelings and how you resolve them.

3. Why is it so hard for us to let go of our "babies," the thoughts and words we create?

4. What are your thoughts about God being your editor? Talk to him about his role in that context.

Penman

The Lord said to me, "Take a large scroll and write on it with an ordinary pen.
Isaiah 8:1

I love gel pens. Their ink flows smoothly from the cartridges onto the paper. Words skate upon the lines with ease. I can use any pen that is handy and full of ink, but when I want creativity, I like to write with my favorite pens.

My friend doesn't like the gel variety. She claims the ink smears. She prefers the old BIC brand. Click it and use it, she says. Just the basics.

Another friend recently delved into artistic lettering and discovered a whole new world of pens with varying tips, widths, and styles. Her collection of colors and purposes for each pen far outnumbers my overflowing baskets of writing tools.

Lord of the Pen, what tools do you want me to use to communicate your message?

Humans have been writing with some type of instrument for centuries. In the year 3500 BCE in Sumeria, the writing system called "cuneiform" developed and people used a stylus to write on clay. The Sumerian region was in southern Mesopotamia, where modern-day southern Iraq and Kuwait are found.

Later in the 6th century, people employed quill pens. The writer first sharpened the feather with a knife, then dipped the end into the ink to fill the empty shaft which served as the ink reservoir.

By the late 1700's, machine-produced steel-point pens arrived onto the penmanship scene. These pens were stronger and could be mass produced, so more people began to use them.

The fountain pen next appeared, followed by the use of a rotating ball to spread the ink on paper. Now more than 2 billion ballpoints pens are made in the United States each year.

God doesn't care what instrument you use to communicate his good news – your voice, a favorite pen, the keyboard, or a plain pencil. As he told Isaiah, "Take out a large scroll and write." Or use your voice if that is your tool to tell his story.

The point is to obey God in our calling as communicators and do the work with whatever tool you like best and fits your communication style. Ordinary or fancy, communicate the message God has given you.

Lord of the Pen, you are the spirit behind every word and the power in every drop of ink on the page. Move whatever instrument we engage to articulate clearly your message to others about your love, grace, and goodness.

1. What is your favorite writing instrument and why?

2. Write out how God has called you to communicate his story and how you are obeying this call.
3. Ask God to lead you into new creativity, new forms of communicating, and fresh opportunities for spread his good news.

Speechwriter

Then the Lord reached out his hand and touched my mouth and said to me, "Now, I have put my words in your mouth." Jeremiah 1:9

Politicians, royalty, and celebrities employ speechwriters to create, style, and format their words to present to the public. Each sentence is carefully crafted with precise selection of the right words, and the rhythms and timing of the entire presentation is staged.

These behind-the-scenes people support the person saying the words and boost their message to the world. They are hired to prepare an address that will be delivered by another person.

The speechmaker furnishes the foundational framework for a message.

Lord, be my speechmaker – the power behind each word I speak and write.

Where do we get inspiration for our words? How does God send us his inspiration for his words?

We connect with God as the source for our inspiration through prayer, time in his word, music, nature, and other inspirational writings. Spending time with God, we listen to his wisdom which constructs and strengthens our foundation as writers and speakers.

The job of a speechwriter behind the visible VIP is essential for their success. The speechmaker interacts with the presenter with open communication and clarity about the message. The deliverer of the message listens and asks questions. The one presenting takes the lead from the creator of the words.

Beforehand and not at the last minute, this relationship builds over time. The speechwriter knows the voice of the one he is creating words for and knows how to make the speech giver communicate in the best fashion true to his/her identity.

As speakers and writers, we pause before writing at the keyboard. We stop before we put the pen to paper to outline the next presentation. We listen to what the Speechwriter is telling us. We prayerfully ask what is the key message God wants us to communicate today. We then humbly ask for the right words, the clear message, and correct tone and color of our statement.

Most of us don't have the luxury of hiring someone to craft our words for us. Wouldn't it be nice to have an outsider provide the words to help you handle that difficult relative? A supportive guide to help us transform readers and audiences with God's message?

For Christian communicators, we do have a speechwriter – God. If we listen, spend time with him, study his word, we will find the resources we need. He will give us the words to spread his good news to others.

Father of all words, may we always turn first to you as we struggle to find the right words and craft the clear sentences to tell others of your love. Open our ears and hearts to hear you, to know you, and to communicate the message you want others to hear and know.

1. Keep track this week of how much time you do spend with the Lord.
2. Write out your prayers in your journal and reread them for wisdom.
3. How has God surprised you when you were working on a speech or writing a piece?

Blogger

Post this at all the intersections, dear friends.
James 1:19 (The Message)

Every autumn, people decorate their homes with fall colors, wreaths bursting with colorful leaves on the front doors, pumpkins and gourds sitting on doorsteps, and a goblin or two in the yards.

Then the stores bring out Christmas decorations. Most of us complain it is too early, yet deep down, we get excited that we will soon celebrate that season.

But one ornament that appears every fall that I could do without is the election sign. Small announcements for school board members and large wooden advertisements for a "much-needed" levy breed like rabbits. Vote no on this issue. Vote yes on that one.

You see a sign promoting Issue 2 and discover something is on the ballot you never heard of before. Then you seek more information to make the best decision.

These posters shout at us to get our attention and to sway our vote. The constant bombardment, though, we complain about it, does work to get us into action and to vote one way or another.

Signs posted at every intersection.

In most communities, we are better at evangelizing political issues than we are telling others about the saving power of Jesus Christ.

Lord, show me how you want me to tell others about you.

A few years ago, many of my writing friends were all starting blogs. I knew nothing about blogging and really didn't think I had the time or talent to write on a blog. Peer pressure won. I became a blogger.

I entered a new intersection and took a turn I didn't expect.

I learned each entry on a blog is called a "post." The correct terminology isn't "I blogged today;" it is "I posted on my blog."

God is always surprising me. I prayed to have him show me a new way to tell others about him and he led me to blogging. Now I do "post" as instructed in this passage from James.

Through posting my spiritual struggles and lessons on my blog, I connect with people around the world in new ways. I renewed old acquaintances and found new friends.

I experienced as a communicator the pressures of having to create something – digging deeper into my life to find nuggets of truth from God – even when I didn't have a clue what I was going to write that day.

I developed better time management skills having a deadline.

I sharpened my observation skills to see God in new places.

Learning to post, not only became an intersection to draw others closer to God, it opened my heart to his lessons too.

Intersections serve two purposes. Most intersections we are called upon to stop or at least slow down and look around. Secondly, we make a decision: go straight or turn, depending on our destination.

I enter an intersection every time I communicate through blogging. I post at that intersection, pausing to listen, to slow down, and then proceed where God leads.

Whether we are writing or speaking, communicators create intersections for our readers and listeners. We post at that intersection. We give them reasons to stop, listen, and then continue their journey.

I never thought before that God might have been the world's first blogger. He posts his message everywhere we look; in nature, in the eyes and the touch of others, in the tragedy of awful news events, in the giggling of a young child, and through us in every word we speak and write.

God, the original Blogger. I like that thought.

Dear Lord of the entire universe, you create all words. you initiate all our thoughts. You are the source of all I think I invent. You are the originator. Be with me as I compile my words into venues such as books, articles, presentations, and even onto my blog. May all my posts – written and verbal – bring glory to you.

1. What have you learned at the intersections of your life? Are you at a crossroads now?

2. Think about God as you cross intersections today in any travel you are doing. What did you learn?

3. The word "post" means to bring public notice to something" or "to publish." What have you posted about God and his lessons in your life?

Biographer

Jesus did many other things as well. If every one of them were written down, I suppose that even the whole world would not have room for the books that would be written. John 21:25

Why do biographies continue to appeal to all generations? What do we learn from reading the stories of other people?

"Jesus did many other things as well." When I read this verse, I wonder what additional wise words Jesus said that weren't recorded for us. What was left out from his life story we read in our Bibles?

Jesus' life on earth is God's biography. God came as Jesus to walk among us and walk in our shoes. He experienced the world from our point of view.

Studying Jesus' story of faithfulness, obedience, and servanthood, we learn how to live life fully. We gain insight and encouragement in how to make better choices, face conflict, and find meaning in life.

The phrase "the whole world would not have room for the books that would have been written" stirs my imagination. I imagine other people he healed physically and transformed spiritually. These words imply many others were changed by Jesus. How does Jesus' story impact our stories?

Lord, help me hear your story and be open to modeling my life after yours.

Biographies provide life lessons through the stories of others. We learn their ups and downs. We walk in their shoes. We experience the world from their personal point of view.

> *When we share our stories, what it does is, it opens up our hearts for other people to share their stories.*
> *And it gives us the sense that we are not alone on this journey.*
> *Janine Shepherd*

Hearing another's story, we gain insight and encouragement in how to make better choices, face conflict, and find meaning in life.

When we read the Bible, we discover the stories of people who lived thousands of years ago yet shared the same struggles as we do.

Their biographies lead us to self-discovery and new perspectives. We see the world differently through the stories of others. We learn as speakers and writers that people's narratives enrich our own stories and when we share them, provide light for others to see their own lives from new angles.

Life stories give us courage to keep trying even through difficult times. When we listen to narratives and read biographies, we are encouraged to persevere and to rise one more time.

Stories help us see the whole picture of life. Our hearts expand with compassion and we reach out so others can fully live their stories. We learn life is not just about us, but about the whole work of God.

Lord of all our stories, you know us well. You sent your son to walk among us to show us the way to you. Open our hearts to learning more about Jesus through his stories from his time on earth and thank you for continuing to invite us into your story and walking with us each day.

1. What lessons have you learned from the biography of Jesus?
2. If your life were written in a biography, what would be the names of each chapter?
3. What are others learning from your life story?

Author

Let us keep our eyes on Jesus the author and perfecter of our faith. Hebrews 12:2

Ever wonder about the word *author?* Our initial reaction may be that an author is just another word for writer, but where did the word originate?

Author comes from the 12th century Old French word, *autor,* and means father. From Latin author can mean originator, creator, instigator, founder, master, and leader. Literally it means "one who causes to grow, to increase" as in the word *"augment."*

An author, like an artist, carefully selects each letter and designs them into words. He dips his pen into the inkwell of words to create sentences and paragraphs that become a story.

The author envisions the plot. The author develops the characters with just the right balance of endearing traits. The author chooses the best setting and adds detailed descriptions for a colorful tale.

The author isn't done yet, for now the editing begins to bring the story to perfection. The author hones each word, every paragraph, and individual chapter.

The author loves his work and his passion oozes into every element.

Lord, you are the Author. Teach me your ways.

As communicators, we acknowledge the divine muse behind any creative idea that emerges as we type or speak. We deeply sense we are not the originator of a tale, a lesson, or inspiration. We keep our eyes on the One who is the Author of the entire universe.

I don't always remember to bow down before this Author and Perfecter. Sometimes I fail to give credit to the One who is the spark of a new idea, the passion behind my words and the engineer of what I think is my design.

Everything begins with God. As communicators, our first action should be to bow our heads in prayer and worship before even starting the next project. He sends the thoughts and ideas for our presentations and writing.

"Every person's life is a fairy tale written by God's fingers."

Hans Christian Andersen

In the end, I hope to enter heaven holding a book that captures my life as a tale written by God. I want his autograph on the front cover and his fingerprints all over every page. Laughing I say to God, "I wonder if there is a Kindle version of the complete book, so I can see it now."

God is the creator of all we do as communicators. Let us keep our eyes only on him, the Author and Finisher of our faith.

Lord I am humbled to realize the depth of what it means to have you the author of my life and the perfecter of my faith. I can barely grasp the meaning that the word "author" means father, creator, and master. you and you alone are the One who causes growth and increase. You continue to edit my life story bringing me to the best finale – heaven with you.

1. How do you use prayer as you begin a new project?

2. What can you do to remind yourself of God as the Author of your life's tale?

3. How is your life different, knowing he is the source, the creator of all words, sentences, and stories?

The Chief Calligrapher

I, Paul, write this greeting in my own hand, which is the distinguishing mark in all my letters. This is how I write. 2 Thessalonians 3:17

I have a basket in my office with special pens and practice sheets to learn the art of creative, beautiful lettering.

I have always been attracted to calligraphy. But, you see, I have little to no natural artistic talent. My lack of fine motor skills messes with my handwriting and stifles my attempts at perfect lettering.

I watch how-to videos and love watching the ink flow gracefully from their pens onto the paper. I have signed up for online courses, which I rarely complete. I envy other people's decorative script and long for this artistic skill.

Alpha and Omega, you are every letter that shapes my life. Show me the lessons that I can communicate with my hands.

Paul wrote the greeting in today's verse using a distinguishing mark. This reminds me of calligraphy. I imagine his unique writing may have matched a sloppy swirl like a doctor's prescriptions, but his handwriting may have also been unique and exquisite.

How we craft our letters reveals more than 5000 personality traits about ourselves. Then we add our tone of voice, nonverbal motions, and vocabulary. Our words become mirrors of our deepest selves. As speakers and writers, we represent God's message to others and we desire to have our words whether spoken or written to reflect God.

Calligraphy is the art of writing beautifully. Honing the skill of calligraphy takes hours of practice, following precise lines. The artist tries different pens and focuses on each detailed movement. Slowly the muscles in the hands learns the patterns and the letters become natural and echo the original.

We too sharpen our communication craft to tell God's story through listening, reflecting, and practice. Over and over we rehearse and edit our material. We spend time with God, hear his word and listen to his voice, so the muscles in our hearts match his heartbeat.

Our scribbles transform into art. Our words wake souls. Our own inner font emerges onto the canvas of creativity under the guidance of the Chief Calligrapher.

Lord of written and spoken beauty, you give each of us a distinguishing mark, a message to communicate. May our words reflect your glory and tell your story.

1. What is your distinguishing mark in your message?
2. What area do you need to practice in order to improve your skills?
3. How would you describe the beauty found in your words?

Speaker

Words satisfy the mind as much as fruit does the stomach; good talk is as gratifying as a good harvest. Proverbs 18:20 (The Message)

Baby babble. They coo with cuteness and we eagerly listen for that first mama and dada.

Ever wonder how a baby learns to talk? How do they begin to understand the meaning of words in such an incredibly short time?

Neuroscientists at the University of Washington asked the question: What happens in the brain that prepares a baby to move from speech perception to speech production?

They used a high-tech machine that tracks millisecond by millisecond the activity of brain cells. Researchers placed babies in this device, which looks like an enormous hair dryer, and then played different sounds to the babies.

What they discovered it that by the age of twelve months, millions of nerve cells in the brain's two language centers are successfully connecting and communicating: first hearing the sound, then producing it. Babies learn to speak by listening first, then practicing. Studies show babies understand many words as early as six months, though they can't speak them yet.

Lord, help me to listen first and then speak.

As communicators, whether through our voices as we speak or through our messages we write, we use words. Proverbs tells us good talk is like a good harvest, capable of feeding many people with healthy food.

Words are powerful. They heal, create, encourage, and change lives.

Words are powerful. They also can hurt, destroy, tear down, and change lives.

We have a God who speaks. God teaches us how to speak. he is speaking all the time.

We need to learn his vocabulary. God speaks with love. We need to listen intently.

The Bible contains many examples of how God speaks.

In 1 Kings 19:12 – After the earthquake came a fire, but the Lord was not in the fire. And after the fire came a gentle whisper.

Psalm 68:33 - To him who rides across the highest heavens, the ancient heavens, who thunders with mighty voice.

Revelation 1:15 - His feet were like bronze glowing in a furnace, and his voice was like the sound of rushing waters.

Our job is to listen. Listen intently, just like babies do when they are learning what words to best use and how to say them best to communicate their full meaning.

Scriptures tell us stories of the people of God hearing his voice.

Abraham heard God tell him to leave the land of his ancestors, and go to a land that God would show him.

Hagar heard God tell her that her son, Ishmael, was also heir to the promise, that he, like Isaac, would be the ancestor of a great nation.

Moses heard the voice of God calling out of a burning bush.

In the story of Elijah, we are told that the voice of God was not in the storm or the earthquake or the fire, but in the resounding silence.

To be effective communicator, we first need to listen. Listen to the One who forms the words and sounds that will nourish our baby brains.

God the Speaker is talking. Are we listening?

Lord, I want the words I speak to glorify you. help me listen to you, learn from you. you model the way for me in all my speech. May my speaking be a full harvest for your kingdom.

1. Study the different Bible verses above referring to the voice of God. How is God inviting you to grow in your speaking?

2. On a scale of one to ten, how well do you listen? What specific steps could you take to strengthen that skill?

3. If you are already a speaker, take out one of your presentations, pray, and update its words.

4. What is one step you could take in the next few months to strengthen your speaking?

Engraver

See, I have engraved you on the palms of my hands; your walls are ever before me. Isaiah 49:16

Ever watch an engraver? Their hands are steady. Their work is precise. They focus only on creating the beauty before them.

An engraver is an artist etching a specific design, word, or image onto a surface. They may use hand tools or a laser, depending on the project. Surfaces may vary from glass to metal to stone to wood to delicate fine paper.

Some engravers work with stencils or a formed design to guide their work to mirror the original. While engraving, he or she will gently wipe or blow away the dust of what doesn't belong. They then sand down the edges to create a beautiful masterpiece.

Divine Designer of all life, steady and guide my hand as I craft the words to tell others of your love.

Isaiah quotes God saying he has "engraved you on the palms of my hands." God is an engraver. What a wonderful image of God to ponder in our conversations with him.

God is steady and complete in his work. He sees you as his work of art, not just inscribing you on one of his hands, but on both palms. He loves you so much, he focuses only on you.

God is an artist, etching a specific model for your life. The Creator slowly shapes you into the image he has in mind for your life.

God is the stencil – you are the design. He forms you with much love and care. The breath of God gently blows away the dust that no longer is needed. He carefully sands down our rough edges. He loves to hold his unfinished masterpiece in his hands, knowing what beauty is still to be revealed.

An engraver's workshop is clean and his tools sharpened and ready to go. We are called to keep our souls clean and the tools of our trade sharpened in the work of the Lord.

As communicators, we are continually being formed by the Eternal Engraver.

Eternal Engraver, thank you for your ever-constant care for us. Form us as you desire and guide us in creating words that draw people to you as their Creator. We rest, knowing we are engraved in the palms of your hands.

1. How do you see yourself engraved in God's hands?
2. Watch an engraver, either in person or on a video, and take that image into your prayers with God.
3. As a communicator, how are you sharpening your tools?

Reporter - God's Stringer

Write, therefore, what you have seen, what is now and what will take place later. Revelation 1:19

I write for our local newspaper. Yes, I am a reporter, but I am more commonly known as a stringer.

A stringer works part time for a paper, often covering evening school board meetings and interviewing people for the profile articles.

A stringer strings bits of info together to make a story – that is how we got our name. We string words together.

Another story about how we got our name says this: Some stringers get paid by the 'inch" that is inches in a newspaper column. At the end of week, the boss measured the inches of the printed stories with a string. They calculated the pay based on the length of the string.

My editor told me one thing as I began this new job: be accurate.

I have learned this lesson the hard way: no one likes his or her name misspelled or the wrong date for an event. And heavens forbid if you misquote them - even though you recorded it and wrote it down word-for-word.

I have learned if I can make someone "look good" in print, they don't care if I slightly misquote them.

I am just a stringer.

A stringer is the low man on the totem pole. We are nobodies, just covering the news the best we can. We write what we see, what we hear, what is happening now, or coming in the future. Still we have our place and we are necessary for getting the word out to other people.

Lord, as a communicator, how can I best get your word into the hearts of others?

I wonder what it would be like to be a stringer for God. Is that what we are as communicators?

How can we best tell God's story? This verse in Revelation gives us three guidelines:

- Write what you have seen.

- Write what is now.

- Write what will take place later.

Write what you have seen.

Writers weave great stories and illustrations that give us easy to grasp images to describe our world. I love reading a sentence where a fellow writer nailed exactly how I felt or what I have seen.

We work on our craft to string the best words together. Our messages are clear, precise, and convey accurately the reality of truth.

Write what is now

Good communicators find the nugget of truth in today's news, give it background from its history, and then expand on the possible options/consequences.

God's reporters look around at today's headlines, issues that impact our readers and give them a perspective on the world. We help others connect God's word to everyday life. Our messages provide the application of his wisdom to our decisions and discussions.

<u>Write what will take place later</u>

Being a reporter for God helps create a framework for the future. We give the foundation and guidelines that assist others in following God. Our messages shed light on the paths we walk.

Lord, you know the past, the present, and the future. You have called me to be a communicator, helping others transition between each phase and to find your presence in. help me accurately find the words that point to you.

1. What type of assignment has God given you to write/speak to others?

2. What do you see happening today that impacts your listener/reader and could be incorporated into your communication?

3. What is one new skill to learn to strengthen your ability to "string" words together for God?

4. How does it change your image of yourself to see yourself as a stringer for God?

Playwright

As he preached he said, "The real action comes next: The star in this drama, to whom I'm a mere stagehand, will change your life. Mark 1:7 (The Message)

A playwright is simply a person who writes plays. Ever wonder why it isn't spelled playwrite?

After all, if you write songs, you are a songwriter. And you handwrite if you use a pencil or pen to create stories and notes with your hands. Logic would have it then if you write plays you should be a playwrite. But the English language often neglects common sense.

The word "playwright" journeys back to the 1600s and the working-class guilds. The origin of this spelling comes not from the sense of a writer, but of a "wright," a construction worker. More than writing a play, the playwright crafts the words and shapes the message.

Maker and Creator, help me see my work as crafting words for you.

Creating a message either in our writing or our speaking, is work. We toil at finding just the right word. We collect stories and dig through ideas to find a gem to share. We tussle with an article or talk to hone it to perfection.

Writing and speaking isn't the glamorous job we see in the movies or imagine it to be. We are craftsmen, not just artists. We sit for hours in front of a blinking curser juggling sentences, hewing paragraphs, and chopping off a well-loved phrase that doesn't fit. We stay up past midnight pruning and polishing the final presentation.

> *There is nothing to writing. All you do is sit down at a typewriter and bleed.*
> *Ernest Hemingway.*

Crafting our message is hard work. As communicators, we too are as much the "wrights," as we are writers and speakers. We are the crafts-persons and builders of books and presentations. We take the tools of our trade and form ideas and discussions that transform thoughts and behavior.

A diamond is a treasure when found. But these gems often need to be cleaned up, shined, and smoothed. Skilled artists with expert hands work the diamond, grind the edges, and bring out its beauty.

A rough diamond holds much potential, but its brilliance and fire emerges in the hands of a patient cutter. Our words also begin as unrefined diamonds. We are both the crafters and the artists of our work.

We are playwrights. We wordwrights. We are speechwrights. We are communicationwrights.

Lord, you are the perfect playwright. Show us how to improve our craft and create the communication you desire us to share. Give us the words to build messages, gather tools to tell

*others, and complete within us the finished
product of our trade.*

1. How do you sharpen your tools as a
   communicator?
2. When have you experienced a "diamond"
   from God that you crafted into a message?
3. What do you enjoy the most about the
   work of writing and speaking?

Spokesperson

If you utter worthy, not worthless, words, you will be my spokesman. Jeremiah 15:19

The number one fear in the United States is public speaking. People are more frightened to give a presentation than they are of death, rattlesnakes, or heights.

In a recent survey, 41% of the respondents listed public speaking as their first fear and only 19% checked the fear of death.

Being a spokesperson is not an easy job. Often a company's spokesperson stands in front of flashing cameras to announce a layoff or the firing of a key person.

The spokesperson for the local fire department speaks to media about the devastation when a home is burnt to the ground. Lives may have been lost.

The spokesperson, also called the press secretary, of the President of the United States fields a wide gamut of questions. he or she must be prepared with accurate, up-to-date information for any situation throughout the world.

Now I do have a confession, I like public speaking. I enjoy creating of the presentation, but I do get nervous just before I go on stage. My greatest fear is not the speech, but spilling black coffee down the front of my white blouse just before I speak.

But giving a talk is different from being a spokesperson. A spokesperson is someone who represents another. They could also be called the voice, the ambassador, or my least favorite, the mouthpiece.

An official spokesperson carries heavy expectations. They possess the skills to choose and to say just the right word. A wrong word could give a different interpretation of the event.

Lord, if I am to be your spokesperson, let my words be worthy of you.

How can we be worthy spokespersons for God?

God appointed us to share his good news with others. We act as his spokesperson. As this verse guides us, we are to utter worthy words, not worthless one.

The birds may sing of God's glory and the rocks can shout out his praises, but we are God's voice to other human beings.

How can we best prepare to be a spokesperson for God?

The key elements are prayer, study, and listening to our fellow Christians for feedback.

Good preparation gives us the credibility to communicate God's truth. Facing our fears and trusting in God's spirit to strengthen our shaking knees, we can face even the most skeptical audience.

The secret?

Focus on the Message, not the messenger.

Lord, I want my words to be worthy of you. When I speak about you and share the good news of

Jesus, may my words penetrate the hearts of the listeners.

1. How does being a spokesperson for God impact your life?

2. How do you prepare yourself to be a spokesperson for God?

3. Where do you find the worthy words?

4. How do you eliminate worthless words in our talk?

Scribbler

Jesus bent down and wrote with his finger in the dirt. They kept at him, badgering him. He straightened up and said, "The sinless one among you, go first: Throw the stone." Bending down again, he wrote some more in the dirt. John 8:8 (The Message)

Scribblers.

You could say some of our handwriting is more lines and wiggles than readable. The medical profession now uses electronic medical records, primarily to reduce the number of errors that occurred due to poor handwriting.

I've seen some people's signatures on legal papers that I could never decipher. I know my own handwriting leaves much to be desired.

A toddler loves to scribble. He proudly scrawls his creation on a paper, and in his eyes he sees his house, his family, and maybe his dog. The sun shines brightly in the upper right corner.

The meaning of a young child's lines, loops, and squiggles are lost on most adults. But the child is trying to communicate something important and share a deep expression.

As parents and grandparents, we ooh and ahh at this work of art and display it on the refrigerator. We may not know exactly what his scribbling means, but we listen and love him anyway. To the stranger, we try to explain what all the lines and colors communicate.

Lord, make sense of my scribblings so its meaning glorifies you.

Jesus was also a scribbler. The Bible doesn't tell us what he wrote in these verses, but he wrote, not once, but twice. He bent down and with his finger, scribbled in the sand. He was communicating something for the others to know.

We wonder if our words – written or spoken – are clear or to others, do they look like scribbles in the dirt. We ask God for help in making sense of our words, our lines, loops, and squiggles.

May our scribblings transform hearts and communicate what God wants in our message.

Dear Lord of all Words, we don't know what you scribbled in the dirt that day, but the fact you wrote, you communicated, you moved hearts and minds to compassion, tells us that even our scattered, scrawling scribbles may be transformational when empowered by you. Make sense of our scribblings for you.

1. Talk with Jesus and imagine what he may have been writing that day in the dirt.
2. Take your prayer time outside and scribble with your finger in the dirt as you talk and listen to God.

3. Free write or speak out loud the message you feel God is giving you. Listen to the words as if they were scribbled in dirt by the finger of God.

Broadcaster

Hear this, nations! God's Message! Broadcast this all over the world. Tell them, 'The One who scattered Israel will gather them together again.
Jeremiah 31:10 (The Message)

I loved listening to WKYC radio as a teenager. My bedroom radio dial sat permanently to 1100 AM. I even kept the music on overnight while I slept. When away from home, I carried a crackling transistor with me, so I wouldn't miss a song or a story.

I knew each announcer's voice – Jerry G, Jay Bird Lawrence, Steve "Boom Boom" Cannon. I could recite their well-known funny lines and even collected their autographs.

My favorite broadcaster was Jim Runyon. One early April morning I heard he died unexpectedly. That day became one of the saddest ones of my teen years. I withdrew for a few hours into my room to cry. My world stopped briefly. I felt like I lost a best friend.

Isn't it powerful how listening to someone on the radio connects to our hearts in a very intimate way? These broadcasters influence our tastes, behaviors, and lives.

I wonder how they do it? How do they build such trust and loyalty?

Effective broadcasters communicate frequently. They talk in the language of their audience. They reach out and invite others into a close relationship.

We respond by listening often. We slowly get to know the broadcaster as a friend.

Lord, I want to broadcast your good news so others come to know you and follow you.

The word *broadcast* originates from the farm fields, meaning the spreading of seeds, such a scattering the seeds in all directions. Radio adapted the word into broadcasting, meaning to spread information widely.

Have you noticed how quickly news spreads?

Recently three high school girls from my area were driving to an away basketball game in the neighboring county. They turned left just as a semi attempted to pass them. Two were unconscious at the scene and in critical condition; the third one texted for help.

While waiting for emergency responders to arrive, she continued to communicate with friends and family through her cell phone.

Other students, already at the game, knew more about what was going on than the rescue squad going to help them.

Twitter, Facebook, cell phones – all have sped up how quickly news is passed. No matter our age, we hear messages almost immediately though these mediums.

Can we use these new technologies to broadcast the news of God too? Can we spread the seed of his Good News all over the world?

The most powerful medium to help us tell the Good News is the Holy Spirit. We can change hearts and lives by connecting first with God's spirit before we link with others though technology. God's spirit helps us share his message.

As God's broadcasters, we use our words to build trust in the Lord. We invite the audience to come alongside of us as we all get to know God better. As we grow closer to God, we recognize his voice and know his stories.

Lord, let my words broadcast widely your message of love and grace. I may never see the impact of the seeds I scatter, but I know your blessing will nurture their growth. May your voice be heard through my voice and your words through my words.

1. How many different mediums do you use to spread the good news about God?

2. What new way can you learn to tell God's story?

3. Identify who has been a positive influence on your faith and study why this impacted you so much?

Composer

He put a new song in my mouth, a hymn of praise to our God. Many will see and fear and put their trust in the Lord. Psalm 40:3

Some people love to write stories, the written word.

Some people love presenting before an audience, the spoken word.

And some people show us God's love through music, the singing word.

For a long time, I asked God why he didn't give me a better singing voice. I wanted to sing for him like Sandy Patti or Amy Grant. To be the soloist. The one lifting his name up while inspiring others.

Yes, this is my ego speaking and the lure of the limelight and fame, but to be honest, I also have a deep desire to draw others to God through music. I like singing and feel God through the tempos and rhythms and words sung.

But I am not a soloist. I am an okay singer, but not a famous recording star. I am a member of the choir, not the featured vocalist.

Keeps me humble.

Lord, let me sing your praises and tell your story in the way that pleases you and in the best way that you have called me.

We have people in our congregation who never sing the hymns. They just stand there. Maybe they don't like their voice. Perhaps someone made fun of them once before when they sang. It's possible they grew up in a family that never sung, so they don't sing.

But I always invite them to at least listen to the words and to hear the message in the hymns. Singing is a form of praying.

> *"Those who sing, pray twice."*
> *St. Augustine*

What are the words telling us about God? Inviting us to ponder? How do the music and lyrics form our prayer? How do the lines in the hymnbook match our needs and desires?

Ultimately God is the composer of all music. God guides the writer, the speaker, and the composer to compile inspirational words and choruses to lift our souls and realign our spirit toward God.

The words of today's verse stirred a composer to create *"a hymn of praise to our God. Many will see and fear and put their trust in the Lord."*

God is the source and the focus of our work. Music is one venue to bring his message to others, to encourage and nurture, and to open hearts to trust and know God.

Creative Composer, thank you for music that draws us closer to you. Give us new songs, spirit-

filled harmonies, and refreshing refrains to glorify you and praise your name. Open our hearts to hear your words through music.

1. How do music and lyrics form your prayer?
2. As a speaker or writer, attempt composing a song about the message God has given you.
3. Take out a hymnal and read some lyrics as prayer.

Storyteller

All Jesus did that day was tell stories—a long storytelling afternoon. his storytelling fulfilled the prophecy: I will open my mouth and tell stories; I will bring out into the open things hidden since the world's first day. Matthew 13:35 (The Message)

Everyone has a story to tell.

Jimmy Neil Smith wrote, "We are all storytellers. We all live in a network of stories. There isn't a stronger connection between people than storytelling."

As communicators, each of us tells stories. We know we connect with an audience most effectively when we find just the right story for our writing or to illustrate a point in a presentation.

"Some people think we're made of flesh and blood and bones. Scientists say we're made of atoms. But I think we're made of stories. When we die, that's what people remember, the stories of our lives and the stories that we told."

Ruth Stotter

Think back about someone you loved who has died. No doubt one of your warmest memories is a story about something they did or said. Often these stories bring us the most comfort.

Most stories start with an individual whose challenges, struggles, and conflicts lead to lessons that connect with others.

Stories are powerful.

Lord, I want to tell your story in the best manner possible. Teach me.

Ever wonder why stories resonate with us?

Stories help us find our way in our journey. They join us to one another so we don't get lost. With stories, we feel a part of something greater.

Stories help us make decisions. Do we turn right or left at the various crossroads in life? Or do proceed straight ahead?

Looking back and recalling the stories in our past gives perspective and meaning to our experiences. When we remember the stories of our lives, often we see the hand of God in areas we thought he forgot us.

Jesus shines as a storyteller. He shared his wisdom and inspiration through telling of the parables. Stories we remember even today.

The verse from Matthew says, "All Jesus did that day was tell stories—a long storytelling afternoon." Wouldn't you have loved to be there? Can't you just imagine what an encouraging thought-provoking and even life-changing event that was!

Jesus used common settings, everyday objects, and local characters. He didn't spoil the punch line unless asked to explain further. One of the most effective storytelling tools he used was to paint word pictures, so the listener saw the story unfold easily.

Jesus must have been an animated storyteller putting himself deep in each story. I bet he peered deeply into each of the listener's eyes as if he was talking only to that individual. He invited the audience members to enter each story and make it their own.

Jesus used words like a skilled craftsman, choosing just the right ones to make his point in a concise yet memorable manner.

He lived his story.

His life, death, and resurrection become our story.

Lord, bless my storytelling with your power and wisdom so to light the way for others to find you. I want to learn from the best – Jesus. Show me the way, Lord.

1. Think of three stories (successes, failures, joys, hurts, lessons) from your life that you could develop into an inspirational illustration.

2. Study Jesus' parables. What can you learn from how he tells stories?

3. Take one of your stories and add more description, word pictures, and powerful picture-words.

4. What is God telling you when you review the stories of your life?

Blueprints

[God is] making known to us the mystery of his will, according to his purpose, which he set forth in Christ as a plan for the fullness of time, to unite all things in him, things in heaven and things on earth. Ephesians 1: 9-10

I fell in love with the home we now live in as soon as I toured it. I remember turning to my husband and whispering, "I want this house. This is home."

All homes though, come with imperfections and a long list of needed updates. One of the most expensive changes we wanted to make was to add whole-house air conditioning. This wish-list item loomed too expensive at first since our new house was built with hot water heat and there were no vents to circulate air conditioning.

We saved our money. The old furnace chugged along, but finally died. The perfect time had arrived to replace the furnace and add air conditioning and the necessary venting.

As we discussed the plan with our contractor, we remembered the former owners left us the blueprints of the house. The contractor was thrilled to have them has a guideline for the current renovation.

A few years later when we updated the kitchen, that contractor also used the blueprints in his planning.

Applying the blueprints of the original plan amplifies any transformation.

Creator God, help me see your holy template in my life.

God created us using a unique blueprint for each of our lives. He formed our structure and designed even the hairs on our heads. He knows how we are wired and activated the beating of our heart.

God is the grand architect of our lives. As the creator of our human blueprint, he continues to shape and renovate the final palace of our lives.

As speakers and writers, we continue to discover our own patterns and distinctive ways of seeing the world. Our words help others see themselves as God created them and encourage them to dig deeper to live as God calls them.

God's living word – the Bible – provides the blueprint, his guiding principles on how to live on this human journey. Using this word, we bring honor and glory to God and transformation to our life that in turn, changes other lives and entire communities.

Without referring to and using this blueprint, we construct misshapen walls and internal air vents that don't work properly. If built incorrectly, the entire structure could collapse.

We may face devastating challenges, but going back to basic with the Master Blueprinter grounds us, gives us direction, and guides our ways.

Thankfully God does provide this template for our lives. We grow and live through changing circumstances and transformational times, knowing the God-given blueprint.

Grand Architect, reminds us daily to follow your blueprint. Transform our hearts and renovate our lives to better serve you with our words.

1. What is the blueprint God has for your life?
2. How do you struggle to see God's bigger plan amidst the uncertainty in the world around you?
3. How have other writers and speakers helped you to follow God's plan for your life?

Agent

I guide you in the way of wisdom and lead you along straight paths. Proverbs 4:11

An agent is a person who acts on behalf of another person. Other words for agent are representative, a go-between, or a negotiator.

In a writer's world, having an agent is a means of finally getting noticed by a publisher, getting a decent book contract, and having someone come alongside you for career development. For a speaker, an agent helps get your name out for larger groups and schedules that keynote address that gives you opportunities to reach others for Christ.

At conferences, we line up to meet with an agent, hoping they see our dream and potential and take us on as clients. We listen to panel discussions on what exactly they are looking for, hoping to find the perfect match.

Finally getting an agent can transform that book proposal to a higher level. Their words of advice, suggestions, and polishing can lead to a published book.

I have read that an agent is a generalist and a writer is the specialist. The agent is the conductor of the whole orchestra while the writer plays the French horn.

Lord, I need an agent for my spiritual journey.

God promises in Proverbs to guide us in the way of wisdom and lead us along straight paths. Sounds like an agent to me.

Many times, on our journey through life we crawl along, deserted, isolated with no sense of direction. Yet God is always with us even when we don't feel his presence.

"Thanksgiving is possible not because everything goes perfectly but because God is present. The Spirit of God is within us—nearer to us than our own breath. It is a discipline to choose to stitch our days together with the thread of gratitude. But the decision to do so is guaranteed to stitch us closer to God.

Attend to the truth that 'bidden or unbidden, God is present'."

Adele Calhoun

God an agent for me? Yes, he is always willing to listen, to put up with my self-pity and whining, to bless me beyond my imagination.

God an agent for me? Yes, he came as the Son of God to be my go-between, my intermediary striking down sin and death.

God, as agent for me? God as Holy Spirit intercedes for me, praying my concerns, desires, known and unknown before God.

God, as agent for me? Gently correcting me, nudging me to take the high ground of love and forgiveness when my ego strains towards revenge.

God, an agent for me? God guides us in his way of wisdom and leads us on straight paths leading back to him.

Agents and their clients are in partnership for a mutual goal. God leads, teaches, and prods our spiritual formation throughout life. We serve him by using our words to honor him and nurture others closer to him.

God an agent for me? He already is!

Lord I want that intense desire I feel at conferences to meet and obtain an agent to be overshadowed by the longing in my heart for you. Thank you for being my agent in all you do for me.

1. How do you define an agent?

2. How does having God as your agent, change your spiritual journey? Are you willing to submit your work and all your heart over to him?

3. What is the goal of your partnership with God?

Dramatist

By his Son, God created the world in the beginning, and it will all belong to the Son at the end. This Son perfectly mirrors God, and is stamped with God's nature. He holds everything together by what he says - powerful words!
Hebrews 1:2-3 (The Message)

The word "drama" originates from the Greek word "dram," meaning to act or to do. Drama brings a story to life before our eyes, usually on a stage or in a book. The audience sees the action, hears the voices, and watches the theme of the drama materialize.

God invites us to be part of his story, his narrative of forgiveness, grace, and love. Our human journey draws us into the discovery of our story within God's story. Our work as writers and speakers is then to help others hear God's story and uncover their own stories. Story upon story upon story.

Heavenly Father, open the ears of my heart to hear your story and guide me in helping to tell others about you.

Throughout the drama of life, the Divine Dramatist sets the stage for his story through characters, their powerful words of dialogue, and the setting and theme of the play.

We meet the major and minor characters that shape our spiritual journey. Their words, both spoken and unspoken, form the dialogue of our life. Dialogue sheds light on the character speaking and the one spoken about, and guides us each day in these interactions.

Through these experiences, we learn and grow in various changing settings, like the different scenes in a play. This influences the emerging of the theme which adds meaning to our life. Our purpose is slowly revealed across time, characters, and settings until the final act.

In a drama, each actor brings his or her own flavor to their role, but all work together so the story unfolds as the dramatist designed. As communicators, we are called to learn our lines and listen to direction so the play sends God's message to our audience.

Divine Dramatist, you are the Word. You create the structure for all life, so your story may be told from one generation to another. Thank you for inviting us into your story, for enriching us through characters, settings, and dialogue. Grant us clarity to know how our story joins your story.

1. What is your story and how is it evolving within God's story?
2. Who are the major and minor characters in your life?
3. How are you using your words to tell others God's story?

Columnist

Our mouths were filled with laughter, our tongues with songs of joy. Then it was said among the nations, "The Lord has done great things for them." Psalm 126:2

When I read or hear the word 'columnist" only one person comes to my mind: Erma Bombeck. Erma was a tremendously funny writer in the 1960s and 1970s. Most of her newspaper columns describe everyday experiences living in a family and running a house.

We clipped her columns, posted them to the front of the refrigerator, and shared them with our friends. She took common situations and embellished them with joy.

With many books to her credit, about 4,000 articles, and a humor column syndicated in 900 newspapers in the United States and Canada, she even found time to serve as the humorist on *Good Morning America.*

What made Erma Bombeck such a beloved and effective columnist?

Her communication strengths were her strong voice and appealing sense of humor. Readers and listeners could easily identify with the everyday circumstances she used in her illustrations.

She could tell a great story, pulling in all our emotions, and making us laugh out loud. We enthusiastically couldn't wait to share with others her latest tale. I would say to my husband, "Listen to what she wrote today."

Erma's writing unlocked our emotions. We laughed. We cried. We shook our heads knowing, yes, we had been there too.

Lord, I want to affect people's lives with your story with the same amount energy and joy, that a good columnist does.

What can we learn from God about being a columnist? Jesus and his parables are great examples. He used personalized real stories from common everyday circumstances. He came alongside his listeners and made them feel a part of every story.

In all of God's stories in the Bible, we can find wonderful illustrations that tickle the senses and intriguing analogies that fill the mind and make us think.

Many of our favorite Bible stories are filled with passion and emotions. Others contain key themes and practical solutions. All hold answers to the questions deep within us.

A good columnist develops a relationship with his or her readers. God wants to connect with us and all of his words seek to engage us.

One of my favorite Erma Bombeck quote is this, "When I stand before God at the end of my life, I would hope that I would not have a single bit of talent left, and could say, 'I used everything you gave me."

Lord, when I stand before you I want to be like Erma – not holding a single bit of talent left – all given for you. Help me learn from you, the Great

Communicator, to best reach others with your message of love, forgiveness, and mercy.

1. When you read the Bible, what do you learn as a speaker and writer about communication?

2. What characteristic of the columnists you read would you like to learn more about?

3. What talent/gift has God given you that you feel you have underused or neglected? How could you begin to develop that skill for God?

4. Do you write and speak with joy?

Conversationalist

I have much to write you, but I do not want to do so with pen and ink. I hope to see you soon and we will talk face to face. 3 John 1:13-14

I hate small talk. I would rather write or present a talk to a group than sit face to face, mingle with a crowd, or "work the room" in a social setting.

Some people thrive with others, drawing life-giving energy from interactions and conversations. For me, give me silence. Books. Solitude.

God communicates in many ways, including through conversations. Even introverts need time in community to hear the voices of others, to receive clarity in discernment, and to listen, learn, and grown.

Lord of all words, remind me often of the value of community as a place where I can increase my understanding of your and of others.

Sharing our words in conversation is both an art and a skill. The skill involves sharpening our listening abilities and asking questions to spark continual discussion. The art emerges by being open to receive, to honor the synergy that arise when it isn't only about one person, and to listen for what isn't being said.

Our writing and presentations are also a form of conversations with our readers and audience. As creatives, we bring the skills we have honed and our artistic competency to best present the message God has given us.

We can also carry these skills into our time with God, the greatest conversationalist. God wants to talk with us. He waits for us for face-to-face time together. He listens, receives openly what we say and invites us deeper onto the sacred ground with him. He knows what we cannot express, holds our tears with compassion, and understands our mistakes and doubts.

Our conversations with God form our speaking and writing and provide a rich foundation to nourish others with our words.

Someday we all will meet God face to face. That moment is beyond our imagination, but I am sure the words will flow like they have never done before. From me. And from God.

Listening Lord, thank you for always being there to hear our words and concerns. Help us listen more to you. We honor our conversations and ask your blessings on our conversations with others through our words and presentations.

1. Think about your conversations with God. Do you listen more than you speak?
2. What are you hearing God say in your discussions with him?
3. How do your conversations with God form your writing and speaking?

Messenger

How beautiful on the mountains are the feet of
those who bring good news, who proclaim peace,
who bring good tidings, who proclaim salvation,
who say to Zion, "your God reigns!"

Isaiah 52:7

Angels have been called God's messengers. The
word *"angel"* comes from the Greek word
aggelos, which means "messenger." The
matching Hebrew word *mal'ak* has the same
meaning.

Angels as messengers bring good news about God
to people.

Angels are mentioned in the Bible nearly 300
times, often in the role of messenger.

Are not all angels ministering spirits sent to
serve those who will inherit salvation?

Hebrews 1:14

But the angel said to her, "Do not be afraid,
Mary; you have found favor with God.

Luke 1:30

Then he lay down under the bush and fell
asleep.

All at once an angel touched him and said,
"Get up and eat."

1 Kings 19:5

Lord, let the words I write and the presentations I
speak communicate your message and your good
news.

How can we be the best messengers for God? The messengers from the Bible demonstrate some of the traits we can adopt.

Angels listen. They keep their ears tuned to God. They let the distractions of the world fade away – which can be so hard for us – and listen to God. As communicators, time spent in prayer, Bible study, and retreats opens our ears to hear God.

Angels obey. They hear God's instructions and simply follow though what they are told. No hesitation. No doubts. As a communicator, too often I let my doubts and second-guessing slow me down or even stop being obedient. I forget my calling– to love God and share his good news.

Angels expel fear and give hope. Our job as communicators is to help others put their focus back on God. God is the story, not us. God keeps his promises and that covenant quiets any anxieties and gives light to the darkest moments.

Angels minister. Angels provide nourishment and comfort. Our words strive for these characteristics too.

A former pastor of mine once told me that every sermon needed to include the story of how Jesus came to save us. Every message should point back to the Good News.

Reading this verse from Isaiah, our words proclaim peace, bring good news, and point to God as the only way. Our message is God reigns in our world and in our hearts.

Lord, open my mouth to tell others your good news of salvation. Let what I write and speak

bring peace that begins and ends in your heart.
Let me be a messenger for you.

1. What does being a messenger for God mean?

2. Review some of your writing or presentations; do they communicate God's good news?

3. How could you deepen your speaking and writing ministry?

4. Rewrite this verse in your own words.

Bookworm

When your words came, I ate them; they were my joy and my heart's delight, for I bear your name, O Lord God Almighty. Jeremiah 15:16

What is a bookworm? A bookworm is a person passionate about reading and study. A bookworm lives in a book. He or she dwells within the words and gnaws on its contents. A bookworm feels at home within the pages.

Bookworms are insects that inhabit and eat the pages of a paper book. These creatures are silverfish, book lice, and beetles. Calling someone a bookworm started out as derogatory – they were calling that person a creepy-crawly bug.

Lord of all, help me remember you created even the tiniest insect. Help me learn the lessons I need by living in your word.

A devil doesn't fear a dusty Bible. God's word provides the nourishment we need as speakers and writers and helps provide food to our readers and audiences.

Our spiritual selves need the fortification of knowing God's story. We prepare a presentation or an article taking in one bite at a time of God's message, savoring it and absorbing its meaning. We digest and allow his word to go deep within us, so we are able to spread his Good News through our speaking and writing to others.

The Bible is healthy nutrition for a communicator.

A Bible that is falling apart, usually belongs to someone who isn't.
Charles Spurgeon

Being a bookworm on God's word also brings clarity to our work, encouragement to our day, and insights to share with others. This joy and peace acts like a flavor booster, the special seasoning, in the banquet of our lives.

Being called a bookworm used to be insulting and offensive, but now we can carry the title of bookworm without shame or discouragement. As writers and speakers, we are bookworms for the Lord -beloved bookworms enjoying and eating God's word.

Creator of all words, you give us your word, sprinkled generously with joy and delight. We take in your word and savor its meaning and guidance as spiritual nourishment. We are your bookworms, Lord, dwelling and devouring your message.

1. Are you a bookworm when it comes to reading the Bible?
2. What are your favorite verses and stories to "digest?"
3. How is your ministry to others being nourished by God's word?

Presenter

He had been instructed in the way of the Lord, and he spoke with great fervor and taught about Jesus accurately, though he knew only the baptism of John. Acts 18:25

"Ta-da!" My two-year-old granddaughter shouts, holding her arms up in victory. She just finished showing off her somersaulting skills performing for me, the proud grandmother.

"Ta-da!" She smiles with enthusiasm, knowing she has the audience's entire attention. I applaud wildly.

Kyla may be only two years old, but she knows how to present.

God has his ta-da moments too. When I see a glorious sunrise or the crisp colors of fall. When I breathe in the smell of a newborn or hold the wrinkled, but experienced hand of an elder. Those are moments when I recognized God's Ta-da!

When God looked at all he created, he said it was good. God continues to create even today and I have to believe as in all his works, he says it is good. That sure sounds like Ta-da to me.

God knows how to present with great fervor!

Lord, you are a great presenter. Show me how I can present you in my words so others may see you clearly.

What can we learn from God as a presenter?

God presents the world and as this verse from Acts says, we should present with great fervor. What is fervor, but another word for Ta-da?

The word *"fervent"* literally means, "to boil," from the Latin word, *"fervere."* Our spirit is to "boil over" as we serve the Lord with intense heat and passion.

Fervor is mentioned in other Biblical verses.

**"Love must be sincere. hate what is evil; cling to what is good. Be devoted to one another in love. honor one another above yourselves.
Never be lacking in zeal, but keep your spiritual fervor, serving the Lord. Be joyful in hope, patient in affliction, faithful in prayer."
Romans 12:9-12**

Fervor is presenting with our entire hearts. How do we keep our hearts on fire for God while presenting?

**Whatever you do, work at it with all your heart, as working for the Lord, not for human masters.
Colossians 3:23**

Prayer and studying God's word fuels our spirit. We pray to be open to his calling and instruction and we nourish ourselves in his Word to keep our zeal for him inflamed.

Passion is a key ingredient to fan the flames of our presentations. Our audiences' lives are impacted when we explain our material with enthusiasm and show why we care for the topic.

When God presents, he engages all our senses. We also can connect by following that trait. Give our audience and readers a visual, story, or metaphor to see, music to hear and something tangible to feel and take home.

Following God as the Great Presenter will add great fervor to our words.

Help me to be energized by the flaming fire of your Holy Spirit as you reside in my heart. May I be wholehearted in what I do for you making the most of every opportunity to give faithful witness to your work in my life and in those to whom I reach for Christ. Keep me from growing weary in service for you so that I will someday see a bountiful harvest in this life most especially in the life to come.

1. How do we add heat to our presentations?

2. What have your learned while thinking about God as a presenter?

3. What *Ta-da* moments have you had in your work as a communicator?

The Word

In the beginning was the Word, and the Word was with God, and the Word was God. John 1:1

Some artists work with clay. Others with watercolors or acrylic paints. Maybe you express your deepest identity though music or dance.

Me? I love words. I enjoy playing with them on paper and compiling them into inspirational presentations. Give me a dictionary or thesaurus and I am content to explore and discover new words. The process of seeing an old familiar word and learning a new insight into its meaning brings me joy. Words are my medium for artistic creation.

Lord, be my first and final Word of each day of my life.

Words help us articulate our faith. Words accompany us on our journey through life, guiding and giving insight to experiences. We describe what we feel and face, and then we discover our faith and foundation.

Words form our identity. We find the names to describe ourselves, our core selves, our roles within families and the community, and how we sort the interactions and interrelationships we meet each day.

Words give us a framework for life.

In the beginning was the Word and the Word was with God and the Word was God.

The Word was and is God. God is the original and foundation for all words. From him sprang the poets and the playwrights. God plants the ideas and inspiration. God shapes the songs and sculpts all beauty. God loves to walk with us in compiling and assembling the structure of a creation we use to communicate the story of his love and grace.

God is the first and foremost Word of all our speaking and writing.

Living Word of God, we bow before you knowing you are the creator who shape all words. Thank you for sharing this love of the word with us so we may speak and write your message to all you place before us.

1. How do you see yourself as an artist of words?
2. What are your favorite words? Make a list of the top 10.
3. When you ponder the title *Word of God*, what do you visualize?

Author Notes

- I am always adding more resources and ideas on my blog, healthyspirituality.org Please subscribe so you don't miss out!

- You also may be interested in the books I write to help you along the way: Whispers, Being with God in Breath Prayers, Spiritual Retreats, a Guide to Slowing Down to be with God, and 40 Voices, A Lenten Devotional. See all my books at healthyspirituality.org/amazon

- Did you find this book helpful? Please take a minute to leave an honest review on Amazon. It is a wonderful way to say thank you to an author.

- Interested in going deeper? Prayer Journaling Course: A Practical Guide to Organize, Prioritize and Energize your Conversations with God. Order the course now for only $12 by going to: https://gumroad.com/products/CqGK

Let's connect and share our journeys together - Beside my blog, you can find me:

My author's Facebook page, https://www.facebook.com/Jeanwiseauthor

Twitter https://twitter.com/Jeanwise

Pinterest https://www.pinterest.com/jeanwise22

About the Author

Jean Wise is a writer, speaker, retreat leader, and spiritual director. She is a contributor author of devotions for four compilations, as well as the author of several books. She has also written numerous devotionals, magazine articles, and newspaper features. You can find her books at healthyspirituality.org/amazon.

Jean is a Deacon at St. Peter's Lutheran Church facilitating adult spiritual formation. She has an active spiritual direction practice including leading group spiritual direction. She is a frequent speaker for gathering and retreats in northwest Ohio.

An RN with her Masters in Nursing, Jean retired from public health in 2006 as the County Health Commissioner to focus on freelance speaking and writing. She discovered her calling to nurture others, as she practiced in nursing, and now as she helps others grow closer to God in her ministry of spiritual direction, writing, and speaking.

Don't Forget to Get the Communicator's Companion Bonus!

Writers and speaker love words. Words are our tools, our bread and butter, the material of our message. We love the swirling taste of a great word on our lips and how the perfect phrase reverberates in another's heart and mind.

I have created a list of wonderful whimsical words I love and compiled them into a **FREE** bonus printable for you.

It's easy to get:

Go to http://healthyspirituality.org/words
Put in the secret password: WORDS
Click to get your inspiration bonus download.
Enjoy my gift to you!